Michael Phelps

ABDO
Publishing Company

Big Buddy BOOKS
Buddy Bios

by Sarah Tieck

VISIT US AT
www.abdopublishing.com

Published by ABDO Publishing Company, PO Box 398166, Minneapolis, Minnesota 55439.

Copyright © 2013 by Abdo Consulting Group, Inc. International copyrights reserved in all countries. No part of this book may be reproduced in any form without written permission from the publisher. Big Buddy Books™ is a trademark and logo of ABDO Publishing Company.

Printed in the United States of America, North Mankato, Minnesota.
092012
012013

 PRINTED ON RECYCLED PAPER

Coordinating Series Editor: Rochelle Baltzer
Contributing Editors: Megan M. Gunderson, Marcia Zappa
Graphic Design: Maria Hosley
Cover Photograph: *AP Photo*: Michael Sohn.
Interior Photographs/Illustrations: *AP Photo*: Mark Allan (p. 15), AP Photo (p. 21), AP Photo, file (p. 19), Mark Baker
    (p. 19), Luca Bruno (p. 15), Gregory Bull (p. 15), Richard Drew (p. 27), Mark Humphery (p. 22), Lee Jin-man
    (pp. 6, 23), Rusty Kennedy (p. 16), David J. Phillip (p. 15), Sipa via AP Images (p. 4), Matt Slocum (p. 25), Mark
    J. Terrill (pp. 11, 16), USOC (p. 9); *Getty Images*: Paul Drinkwater/NBC/NBCU Photo Bank via Getty Images
    (p. 29), Ronald Martinez (p. 10), JAVIER SORIANO/AFP (p. 13).

Cataloging-in-Publication Data

Tieck, Sarah.
  Michael Phelps: the greatest Olympian / Sarah Tieck.
    p. cm. -- (Big buddy biographies)
  ISBN 978-1-61783-753-1
  1. Phelps, Michael, 1985- --United States--Biography--Juvenile literature. 2. Swimmers--United States--Biography--Juvenile literature. 3. Olympics--Juvenile literature. I. Title.
  797.2/092--dc22
  [B]
                            2012946489

Michael
Phelps

Contents

Record Breaker

Michael Phelps is a famous swimmer. He has won races at the Olympics, the World **Championships**, and the Pan Pacific Championships.

People consider Michael the greatest Olympian. He has won 22 Olympic **medals**. That is more than anyone else!

Hilary, Debbie, and Whitney (*left to right*) often attend Michael's races.

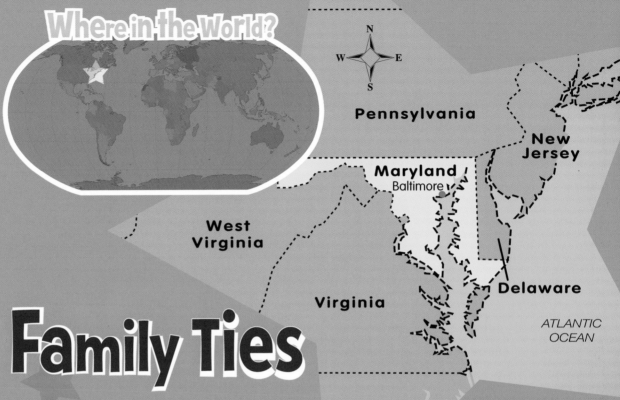

Pennsylvania

New Jersey

Maryland
Baltimore

West Virginia

Virginia

Delaware

ATLANTIC OCEAN

Family Ties

Michael Fred Phelps was born in Baltimore, Maryland, on June 30, 1985. His parents are Fred and Debbie Phelps. His older sisters are Hilary and Whitney.

When Michael was nine, his parents divorced. Life changed for Michael and his sisters.

Early Years

School was hard for Michael. Other kids often picked on him. During elementary school, his family discovered he had **ADHD**. This made learning harder for Michael.

Michael started swimming at age seven. At first, he was afraid to put his face in the water. So, his **coaches** taught him to float on his back. Soon, he could do the backstroke. From there, his swimming skills grew.

Growing up, Michael went to school near Baltimore. He graduated from Towson High School in 2003.

Bob was Michael's coach throughout his swimming career.

Starting Out

When Michael was 11, he began working with **coach** Bob Bowman. They trained every day in Baltimore. Michael worked on the four types of swimming strokes for racing.

Sometimes Michael didn't want to train. But Bob pushed him. He noticed Michael's special body features and swimming skill. He believed Michael would become a great swimmer.

Big Dreams

In 1996, Michael watched the Summer Olympics in Atlanta, Georgia. He saw famous swimmers from around the world.

Michael wanted to swim in the Olympics, too! So, he trained hard. In 2000, he raced in the Summer Olympics in Sydney, Australia.

In 2001, Michael became a **professional** swimmer. He raced in events all over the world. He won **medals** and broke records. People began to notice him.

Michael won four gold and two silver medals at the World Championships in 2003.

The Olympic Games

The Olympic Games are a famous worldwide sports **competition**. The Olympics happen every two years. They change between the Summer Olympics and the Winter Olympics.

People from countries around the world compete to win Olympic events. First-place winners receive gold **medals**. Silver medals are given to second-place winners. And, third-place winners receive bronze medals.

Swimming takes place during the Summer Olympics. Other summer sports include gymnastics and track and field.

Speed skating and skiing are two sports at the Winter Olympics.

Michael won many races in Athens. People compared him to record-breaking swimmer Mark Spitz.

Michael won medals and set records for speed at the 2004 Olympics.

Olympic Champion

In 2004, Michael raced in the Summer Olympics in Athens, Greece. He was outstanding! He won six gold and two bronze medals.

After the Olympics, Michael moved to Ann Arbor, Michigan. There, he attended the University of Michigan. He also continued training with Bob.

Michael was excited to swim at the 2008 Olympics.

Swimming Sensation

In 2008, Michael went to the Summer Olympics in Beijing, China. He planned to swim in eight events. His **goal** was to win eight gold **medals**. No one had ever won so many gold medals at a single Olympics.

In 1972, Mark Spitz won seven Olympic gold medals for swimming. Michael wanted to win eight to set a new record.

Michael was proud of his success at the 2008 Olympics.

At the 2008 Olympics, Michael swam 17 races in nine days. Swimming in so many different races is very **challenging**.

Many races were close. But, Michael reached his **goal** and won eight gold **medals**! He also set seven world records.

A New Dream

After the 2008 Olympics, Michael swam most days to keep his body strong. He continued to win races around the world.

But, Michael had another **goal** in mind. He wanted to win more gold **medals** at the 2012 Summer Olympics in London, England.

Michael had to try out for the 2012 US Olympic swim team.

The 2012 US Olympic swim team had 24 men and 25 women. Some team members posed for pictures before the Olympics.

At the 2012 Olympics, Michael won four gold and two silver **medals**. His last race as a **competitive** swimmer was a team race. Team USA was in second place. But with Michael's help, they gained the lead!

Michael won his 18th Olympic gold medal! This was his 22nd Olympic medal overall. No other Olympian has won so many medals!

Michael was honored for his new record at the 2012 Olympics.

Michael's mother is one of his biggest fans. She is proud of her son.

Out of the Water

Michael's swimming skill has made him world famous. He has appeared on magazine covers and television shows.

Michael uses his fame to help others. In 2008, he set up the Michael Phelps Foundation. This group works to **promote** swimming and healthy living.

THE ALL-TIME OLYMPIAN MICHAEL PHELPS

Sports Illustrated

Buzz

After the 2012 Olympics, Michael said he was done with **competitive** swimming. He was very proud to have reached his **goals** as a swimmer. Now, Michael plans to do more work with the Michael Phelps Foundation. He also wants to travel and see the world. Fans are excited to see what's next for Michael Phelps!

Snapshot

★**Name**: Michael Fred Phelps

★**Birthday**: June 30, 1985

★**Birthplace**: Baltimore, Maryland

★**Turned professional**: 2001

★**Olympic medals won**: 18 gold, 2 silver, 2 bronze

★**Championships**: Olympic Games, World Championships, Pan Pacific Championships

Important Words

ADHD attention-deficit/hyperactivity disorder. A condition in which a person has trouble paying attention, sitting still, or controlling actions.

challenging (CHA-luhn-jihng) testing one's strengths and abilities.

championship a game, a match, or a race held to find a first-place winner.

coach someone who teaches or trains a person or a group on a certain subject or skill.

competition (kahm-puh-TIH-shuhn) a contest between two or more persons or groups. To compete is to take part in a competition.

goal something that a person works to reach or complete.

medal an award for success.

professional (pruh-FEHSH-nuhl) working for money rather than for pleasure.

promote to help something become known.

Web Sites

To learn more about Michael Phelps, visit ABDO Publishing Company online. Web sites about Michael Phelps are featured on our Book Links page. These links are routinely monitored and updated to provide the most current information available.

www.abdopublishing.com

Index